Not Exactly Life

This second poetry collection features women in a variety of guises. You will meet women from life, from fiction, from history and from film.

All of these women have been chosen because for some reason or other they have been influential; perhaps it was a word spoken, or a look given, or a trait possessed, perhaps it was none of these or all of them, but somehow, somewhere, they left their touch with me.

Some you will know, others will be strangers to you but I do hope that you enjoy meeting them.

Margaret Holbrook

Not Exactly Life

Margaret Holbrook

Empress Publishing

With Thanks

to

Phil and Mady

The author aged about 8 months.

Contents

FROM LIFE

FROM FICTION

FROM HISTORY

FROM FILM

FROM

LIFE ...

My Mum

taught me
to keep some independence,
not to be reliant on anyone;
not even those you're closest to.

My mum
taught me how to choose rabbits and poultry,
to skin, pluck and draw the same;
to cook substantial English fare.

My mum
taught me to bake cakes, bread and pies;
to do my own smaller versions for Dad
who enjoyed them, because *I'd* made them.

My mum
taught me to make *Cut and Come Again Cake,*
best savoured warm and spicy
from the oven, loved by older brothers.

My mum
taught me how to wire plugs and change fuses.
To do bits and bobs of men's work;
because men aren't reliable, not really.

Ada, aged Four Months

Written in your mother's
hand on the back of the
photograph. A studio portrait.

You're intent on watching
something; *the photographer?*
And your brown eyes

are fast on him. A good thing,
it kept you still
and you didn't blur the image;

you didn't have to go
through the whole thing
again, be placed 'as you were'

on fur rug and frilled cushion.
There is a choker at your neck.
Stones and pendant both

impossible to make out.
I wonder was it a gift
from parents or grandparents?

Or was it only worn
for the occasion? There's no one
to ask; was it even mentioned?

But then, did I always listen?
Only now do I realise the limit
of my knowledge,

only now, when any
questions are too late.

Mother in Law's Tongue (or a visit to the fish restaurant)

If this is in the window,
my wish is,
my mother in law sees it.
I'll tell her she must visit,
even if it's not her week.
I'll tell her they're cooking
a fish with her name on it.
'Jean,' it will say when it
arrives at the table,
'Jean, eat me, I'm yours.'
But the words would be spelt
out in chips and punctuated
with peas. And she would
sprinkle the dish of words
with salt, to remind the fish
of the sea, and vinegar
to give the chips and peas bite-
and, she would enjoy.

Buying Eggs

I walk from the brightness of the parlour
along an endless darkness to the front door.
Percy stands, basket on arm.
He doffs his cap, smiles, takes the dish
but I choose the eggs.
It's our Tuesday ritual.
Job done, I hand him the money,
wrapped in a piece of paper.
'Correct', he says, and is gone.
I carry my cargo carefully, retracing the steps
I have taken only minutes before.
Now, the eggs will be examined by
Grandma's expert eye and hand.
Only the best, she will say, *only the best.*

Grandma o' Clock

You could set your day by her.
8a.m.: breakfast
12 noon: lunch
4p.m.: afternoon tea
8p.m.: supper.
And so it was, day on day.

And the advancing time was marked
by a change of dress;
plain in the morning, at lunch-time
something with lace collar and cuffs.
At 2p.m. she would rest, descending
the stairs an hour later in her '*afternoon frock*'.
As supper approached, I remember it was
always something '*vaguely navy*'.

Into her eighties, her hair was still long
and was worn *up*, fastened with pins.
A childhood *me* found this fascinating and
after supper, I would sit transfixed in the
dim light of the cottage, watching
as Grandma plaited her hair, knowing
that when the ceremony was finished
it would be bedtime – mine.

The Day The Birds Stopped Singing

The news hit me, shattered the sunlight
turned the day from bright to dark;
Aunty Vee had died.

Mr. Quayle let me go home;
it was half past two,
we generally worked until six.

On the journey home I thought of my Aunty.
I remembered the last time I'd seen her,
just a few days earlier in hospital.

I pictured her, then, covered by white linen
in a bed of *NHS* cream; the sun streaming
through the windows while all the time

outside the birds were singing.
'Listen to that blackbird,' I'd said, and
she'd smiled.

Passengers

The bus rumbles, tumbles my thoughts.
Aunty Marjorie is considered.
The one I never knew.

Settling for the journey, I watch
as other passengers board.
She has skin dark as black-coffee,
hair with the blue-black tints
of a raven's wings.

The boy is busy putting
his back-pack on the seat.
He is smiling.
He has his mother's eyes.

At the ring of a bell, we stop.
Mother and son depart;
still smiling,
a journey ended.

Distracted for a long moment, my
thoughts again tumble.
Years earlier, other travellers.
Aunty Marjorie and her *Indian Army Officer*,
coming home to England.

I picture them together,
happy, smiling.
My uncle and his young bride
from Assam.
Aunty Marjorie,
the one who died too young.

August 2008. A Snapshot

Your 16 year old self smiles
at me when I wake.
Your life is just beginning.
Your long, chestnut hair
newly permed.

I know the dress you're wearing
was a different colour. You told me.
On the photo it's petrel blue;
in reality, cerise.

Your hopes and dreams
spanned over 50 years
of marriage and three children,
yet condenses into objects that
fill a room.

And when we cleared the house,
took things as mementoes,
split up your treasures,
we wanted your approval, still.
We knew that our memories
were the true bonds, knew
that simple things
have more than face value.

Geggy

You'd see her wearing blue or lilac;
alone after fifty and more years.
She kept her garden neat.
Popped up from nowhere;
hour-long conversations were short.

Monday afternoon she went folk dancing.
Her daughter said, 'It'll keep you active.'
'I'm packing it in,' she said, 'I'll not tell Carol.'
She didn't tell Carol she was moving.
Carol saw the 'ad', and then the 'flag',
tried to reason with her mother.

Miss S

wore pastel coloured costumes,
kept her hair in a loose chignon,
wore pearls.
During Art, she would tell us
of her younger life;
have us hanging on her every word.

She allowed me to try woodcarving
praising my attempts,
taught me to love art for itself, and
for the expression of the same.

When she read to the class from
My Family and Other Animals,
two dozen girls were transported to Corfu;
she liked my pastel of the *Rose Beetle Man.*

Sometime during fourth year she left.
We never saw her again;
only overheard tales that wrapped themselves
around school corridors and cloakrooms;
tried to pick out the truth from the gossip.
Art could never be the same
but then, neither were we.

Chester Zoo

A school trip for first years;
a day to explore, in groups of four;
but we were three, so
Miss Oakes came with us.

'Have you seen the vultures?
Very interesting birds, you know.'
We remained silent, looked blankly
at our hair-netted teacher.
Miss Oakes came with us.

Freedom 1971!

We'll start now.
Lizzie calls round
and Jo and Bev.

We go to Bev's,
her mum works.
Radio full blast.

Tami Lynn
damages
our hearing
and that of the
whole street –
probably.

We dance along;
it's going to be
a great summer!

FROM

FICTION ...

No-one Heard a Cry
(after Oliver Twist by Charles Dickens)

It was at night, at home,
when it happened.
He beat her to death;
he was drunk and loud.

She couldn't think he would
really hurt her, not so bad;
not so bad as to kill her.

Warned her, they did;
she just smiled, you see
they didn't know him,
couldn't know him and his ways
or how caring he could be.

And she was loyal, wasn't she?
That was the truth, but
he believed different,
knew different, knew Nancy
for what she was;

he'd been told ...?
And that telling
sowed the seed that
ate him up inside,
the seed that sealed her fate.

She'd turned on him,
hadn't she?

And so it happened,
and not without remorse
he left her.

Emma   *(after Madame Bovary by Gustave Flaubert)*

With another man
things would be different.
I imagine my perfect life.

A handsome husband,
intelligent and distinguished.
We should live in town and enjoy
the noise and bustle of the streets.
We would walk along with
the theatre-goers, the dancers.
I would be in heaven!

We should take tea in
the brightly lit cafes.
And friends,
we would have influential friends.

Instead I am here, trapped,
constrained.
The wife of a provincial doctor.

EMMA *(after Madame Bovary by Gustave Flaubert)*

Avec quelqu'un d'autre
tout serait différent.
J'imagine une vie parfaite.
Un mari élégant,
intelligent et distingué.
Nous vivrions en ville, au milieu
du bruit et de l'agitation des rues.
Nous flânerions, coude à coude,
avec les amateurs du théatre,
les danseurs.
Je serais au septième ciel!
Nous prendrions du thé dans
des salons de thé à la mode.
Et des amis!
Nous aurions des amis importants,
des amis qui comptent.
Au lieu de cela,
je suis ici, prise au piège,
emprisonnée,
la femme d'un médécin de campagne.

FROM HISTORY ...

In the Making

Removed from city centre poverty
this home and garden would have been a paradise.

I pause in the hall, its vastness,
imagine other visitors;
Charles Dickens,
Charlotte Bronte,
John Ruskin,
those from William's chapel.

A stage is set;
a Paisley jacket
a wedding veil,
small treasures of a life.

This home provides
a glimpse of the past.
A snapshot from a time
imagined through
books, documents,
drawing-room fabric.

You, Elizabeth, possessed a need
to write; to expose the vulnerable
to show society's divide.
Mary Barton,
North and South,
Ruth.
The lost,

The underdog,
The weak.

Two hundred years on,
the divide is still with us.

Elizabeth Gaskell's house is at 84, Plymouth Grove,
Manchester

Open to the public

www.elizabethgaskellhouse.co.uk

Finally A Queen

Elizabeth carried herself tall
escaped the stocky, Tudor build.
Here was a woman who wouldn't be put down;
a woman destined to do
a man's job in a man's world
and succeed.
Elizabeth, a girl for all seasons.

Her father would never see this, never
utter words of encouragement and appreciation
for how majestically she governed; but
perhaps he would have been pleased
knowing she had inherited
a steely resolve, learned her craft well.

So, this woman of twenty-five
was no longer a disappointment
for not having been born a prince,
and there would be no regrets at his declaring,
'Elizabeth, daughter of the King of England.'

Miss Borgia

Lucrezia, your family would have kept
the typesetters busy, filling the columns
of *Nascita, Matrimonio, Morte.*

Machinations of the pope, your father;
a fallen cardinal, your brother;
and your life was not your own.

Their murderous scheming kept Rome on its toes,
left nothing to chance, left no one to say
'there but for the Grace of God.'

They had everything in their favour,
the church and you, a bargaining tool
to be reused as long as time and youth allowed.

How long before beauty fades?
Does widowhood and childbirth add years to a face?
Add flesh to once slim bones?

Don't age, don't grieve at the loss they contrive for you;
the one that will right all their wrongs.
Cesare has paved a way to Ferrara, your brother has

spied a rare catch and rich pickings;
the pope offers consent and your future beckons.
Alfonso waits, what they have done?

Their end game wasn't planned,
neither thinks they will lose you,

you *will* return to Rome, Lucrezia, won't you?

The hacks are waiting, clamouring for news,
 is it a boy or a girl? Are mother and child well?
Clicheed phrases that roll off the tongue

are tripped out, but you don't hear them,
and these voyeurs will see in a husband's face
that it's true, you've gone;

left Ferrara, but not for Rome,
and tomorrow?
Tomorrow this news will be history.

After Lucrezia's death Alfonso wrote, *'I cannot write
without tears, so grave is it to find myself deprived of
such a sweet, dear companion as she was to me, for her
good ways and for the tender love there was between
us'.*

East Anglia 61AD

Aged 8, I never tired of this game
the one we played after school.
Anne and Susan would be my daughters,
Lynn, always the horse;
(but nonetheless vital
when you've a chariot to ride).

And me?
I was the warrior queen Boadicea
urging my people to fight on,
not kowtow to the Romans -
but to no avail,
for after many brave battles,
we, the Iceni, were defeated.

The game always ended like this,
(but then you can't rewrite history.)
Anne, Susan and myself would drink 'pretend' poison;
dramatically falling on the grass in the
throes of death, allowing Lynn to run free.

Long moments would pass
then it was tea-time;
my friends all leaving,
allowing me to walk down a path
nineteen hundred years in the making.

The Arts and Crafts Movement

It went with the territory and I think
she wore it well, her dress of ink.
The butterflies, lions, trees and verses,
intricately, intimately shown.
She was unstoppable,
twirling and contorting from a circus trapeze,
this was how *Maud Wagner* could
delight her audience, would hold them
spellbound but gasping for more.

At the end of her act she would
receive rapturous applause, her head
held high on five strands of pearl choker.
Her craft was learned and measured.
Her body a gallery's art displayed,
and at the tattoo parlour, she could
see a queue already forming.

A celebration of Maud Wagner, circus artiste and
travelling tattooist.
Born February 1877, Lyon County, Kansas
Died January 1961, Lawton, Oklahoma

Dolly Shepherd – Aviatrix

From
Alexandra Palace waitress to Fairground entertainer
to Queen of the Air at seventeen –
and all on a whim.

You held the trapeze
as it swung below the
hot-air balloon –
ascending to 4,000 feet
wearing a high flier's costume
and knee high boots,
your long hair held in place under a beret;
from where it never seemed to stray.

You were a natural,
just what the Showman ordered;
never missing a trick
from your lofty position
somewhat higher than a skylark
might fly;

your grip held you there
without glue or trickery;
until, at the correct moment
you loosed the trapeze
from your grasp,
released the cord
parachuted down and waited,
for the next time.

Elizabeth (Dolly) Sheppard/Shepherd 1887-1983
Dolly made her first parachute jump at 17 and retired at
25.

Emmeline

You did so much for your home city
in a time of want and need,
because
you fought for women's rights
for their suffrage
manned soup kitchens
rallied women to your cry;
knew that education
was the doorway from poverty,
and
in Manchester, by the Infirmary
where your house stands
a memorial to you
I now stand and consider,
my thoughts focused
on
the White Feather Campaign,
on those men in reserved occupations
the serving men at home, recuperating
those returned from war damaged,
who needed no reminders of
battles, bullets, death and honour;
those who never would tell
of what they'd seen
and
I wonder, did you think at all
about these men, about their work;
or know anything of the effects of shell-shock
and wounds that couldn't heal?
And

did you care about the boys
going off to be warriors
for a promise of dental care,
hot meals, a uniform?
Did you consider the impact you had
as you handed out your
symbols of cowardice
to those you believed 'lesser mortals?'
But
you see, your life was lived differently.
Perhaps you never struggled with want
even in a time of need, and
you had only your own ideals
to judge others by;
so,
maybe the benchmark was out of kilter
the bar set too high for others to reach,
the paradigm flawed.

The Pankhurst Centre,
62, Nelson Street, Manchester

Open to the public

www.thepankhurstcentre.org.uk

A Suffolk Tale

She went to meet her lover
In the old red barn,
He loved her, he would marry her,
Never do her harm.
Leaving her young son
With her parents
(he cried to see her go)
She left to meet Mr. Corder,
He was waiting for her now.
Corder was the village squire,
He cheated and he lied.
His father tried to change him,
But young Corder he was wild.
Maria loved him dearly,
They had a child, a son,
But for some or other reason
He was dead within twelve months.
'She's no better than she should be'
The village gossips said
Maria just ignored them,
Turned her heel and tossed her head.
'Why meet him now?' her mother said,
'It's late, why should you go?'
William will be waiting,
Please mother, don't fuss so.
'And dressed like a man,
I don't understand,
'What's the idea of that?'
It's so we can travel unhindered.
Free and easy, without a care,

And look, I've William's green kerchief
To fasten in my hair.
I must go now to meet him,
To make a start on life
And tomorrow we'll be in Ipswich
And I'll become his wife.'
Her parents felt uneasy
As they watched their daughter go
But Maria was so happy,
How were they to know?
Later, Corder returned from Ipswich.
But he returned alone.
Spun a tale to the Martin's
And went to his father's home.
'A dream I've had', her mother said,
'I want you to go to the barn,
See if you can find Maria,
I'm sure she's come to harm.'
Her father was less worried
And told his wife to wait.
He'd speak to William Corder
And set the record straight.
Corder wasn't at home
When old Martin went to call.
He'd left, gone back to Ipswich,
Was the master of a school.
Mrs Martin couldn't settle,
Her dreams kept her awake,
Told her husband to check the red barn,
The key to their daughter's fate.
As soon as the barn door opened,
Martin saw soil upon the floor.

Someone had been digging there,
Old Martin dug some more.
There he found his daughter,
The apple of his eye,
Tossed in the earth without a care,
Choked and left to die.
Around the neck of his darling girl
Was a kerchief green and bright.
It was the one she'd tied in her hair
Upon that fateful night.
The police sergeant was sent for,
He gave Corder a call,
Found he had a 'new' wife,
Who helped him at the school.
Taken back to Bury St. Edmunds
Corder was tried and he was hanged.
The Martin's had lost their daughter
By the wicked Corder's hand.
Their beautiful, tragic daughter,
Maria Martin was her name,
Who went to meet her lover
Down a lovers' lane.
And on that late spring evening
In the merry month of May,
Maria Martin met her killer.
William Corder was his name.

Maria Martin was murdered by William Corder on the
18th May 1827.

Her body was discovered by her father on the 19th April 1828, she was 26 years old.
Her remains are buried in St. Mary's churchyard, Polstead, Suffolk.

Nothing Like Belle Starr

I'm nothing like you, Maebelle Shirley
nothing like Belle Starr,
even so, I longed to be like you
a gun in either hand;
firing into the air, riding into town.

Dressed in white, I'd be a picture,
cowboy hat upon my head;
guns drawn from rhinestone holsters
but I'd never shoot another dead, so
I'm nothing like you Maebelle Shirley,
nothing like Belle Starr;

an outlaw's wife and widow,
the girl a father and mother can't understand,
their help decried and scorned, they watch,
as you continue your spiral down.

Robbing, cheating, stealing,
is your way of having fun;
put in the *house of correction*
and when your time is done,
you change, hurrah!
Thank one, thank all,
but the change is forgotten when
the James' gang comes to call.

Later, you take Sam Starr's name,
for better or for worse,
he loves you then he leaves you
when he's caught by the bullet's curse.

But hey, Jim July's waiting,
he's asking for your hand
won't you give your answer Belle?
I'm sure he'll understand; and
perhaps you'll take your time Belle,
but don't look back, there's something planned.

Too late! They've set an ambush;
you've been taken by surprise and
though they say the devil spares his own
you've met your assailant's eyes.

The legend of your shooting star
cascading blood-red all around;
death comes walking quietly
as dear Belle Starr falls down.

Hollywood portrayed you, Belle,
glamorous, generous, bright;
but the truth we know has far more grit
Belle Starr is murdered, pays the price.

I'm nothing like you Maebelle Shirley,
Nothing like Belle Starr.

Belle Starr was born February 5th 1848 and was shot and
killed February 3rd 1889.

Edith

Her mother's *changeling.*
Her father's *plain girl.*
Alone in the company
of mis-matched parents.
A child with words and letters
for playmates;
knowing she was second-best
in a world ideally suited to
first-born sons.

A strange, confusing
childhood giving way to
exuberance, the poet
set about her task in earnest.
Words of wit, wisdom, honesty,
revealing what was seen,
but not known to be seen.
She laid claim to her territory,
took it, grasped it; holding it firm
in slim, alabaster-white hands.

Edith thought it better to, *be oneself.*
Said that she, *wasn't born for fashion.*
Little matter. She had a style
all her own. Jaunty, lively,
flamboyant, and she
carried it off as only she could,
impeccably–
right down to her silver-painted
finger tips.

Edith Sitwell, poetess and writer, born 1887, died 1964. Family home Renishaw in Derbyshire.

Open to the public

www.renishaw-hall.co.uk

St Margaret: The Last Anglo-Saxon Queen

Margaret, the perfect queen,
happy in Scotland, at ease with Malcolm
whose rough edge she polished
diamond-bright until it shone.

Margaret, whose good works cannot be forgotten
offered everything, gave freely,
nursed grown men through final battles
heard last words from whispering lips
grieved at the loss of loved ones.
Died of a broken heart.

FROM

FILM ...

What I Wanted

I wanted to dance like Ginger
when she was with Fred.

I wanted to glide in lacy froth and
silk georgette while the band played on.

I wanted to fly down to Rio, get caught
in the rain on a lovely day.

I wanted all this, but even Miss Vernon's
ballet and tap class for three hours on a
Saturday morning brought no improvement.

I managed only to dance my way to the chorus,
pretend I was, *all yours in buttons and bows,*
while wearing fetching blue gingham.

I received no accolades, no badges of merit;
gave up dancing. Left my silver-screen dreams
for others to pursue.

E.S. Meets M.M.

She thought,
she's like a daffodil
in that green dress
with her golden hair.
Very beautiful and
quiet, thoughtful,
not at all showy.
She has intelligence,
grace, a quiet dignity.
A very nice girl.

Edith liked her almost immediately.
Contrary to what the papers believed or wanted.

She thought,
they treated her shabbily
the press; not realising
what it's like to be hungry.
And all because of some
nude photographs on a calendar.
'Photographs have nothing to do with morals.
That's what the press find confusing.'

Edith liked her; thought her the perfect lady.
And her husband, Arthur Miller;
Edith thought they were both charming.

She thought,
she'd like to meet them again,
perhaps in New York,

the daffodil girl and her husband.
The girl who had been reading
Rudolf Steiner; the girl whose husband
wanted her to play more serious, dramatic roles.

Edith Sitwell first met Marilyn Monroe in Hollywood in
1953, and in London in 1955.

Harlean Carpentier

At home you were Baby Jean;
loved by a mother who worshipped every inch
of the ground you trod, lived off your earnings,
bought houses, kept husbands.

On screen you were the woman
every man wanted but didn't get.
You were the brash tart, the siren,
the girl with an answer for everything.
You had it all, yet somehow life betrayed you;
leaving you on the sidelines with
no chance of getting back.

It might have been different;
you could've married William Powell,
had your own 'happy ever after';
the kind of ending you see on screen;
but Jean,
there would be no final applause;
only a silence you would never hear.

Ill, you left the the studios early,
you left the cameras,
the crew and Clark Gable
on the set of *Saratoga*,
went home to Mama Jean
who prayed,
believing faith was enough.
And then she built a maternal barricade,
excluded friends until it was too late;

too late for jokes and reading *Gone With The Wind.*

William Powell said his final goodbyes.
Laid you to rest with lily of the valley and gardenias.
Grieved for what he might have known and
for what he never would know.
You were twenty-six,
too young to take a final bow.

Jean Harlow was born in March 1911 and died on
June 7th 1937
Gone With The Wind was left unread on her bedside
table.

What's New with You, Kid?

Your path was mapped, the zany brunette dancer who
became blonde before finally settling on the red hair
that no-one else could wear so well.

Line perfect you never ad-libbed
nothing was left to chance, it coudn't be,
you wouldn't allow it.

The American dream was yours
there were no problems, no conflicts.
In TV town the sun always shone.

Desi and Lucy summed up perfection,
completed the happy families set of four
with a pigeon-pair;

but perfection isn't always what it seems,
realisation dawns,
everything, including the marriage is gone;

and you? You did what you had to,
made a go of *Desilu,* sprinkled it with your magic
gave us a weekly dose of *Star Trek..*

You were no longer the tongue-tied girl
from Jamestown, New York. You were a star,
no wonder, Miss Ball, that everyone loved Lucy.